COLONIAL ÉLITES
Rome, Spain and the Americas

THE WHIDDEN LECTURES
January 1958

COLONIAL ÉLITES

Rome, Spain and the Americas

RONALD SYME

LONDON
OXFORD UNIVERSITY PRESS
New York   Toronto
1958

Oxford University Press, Amen House, London E.C.4

GLASGOW NEW YORK TORONTO MELBOURNE WELLINGTON
BOMBAY CALCUTTA MADRAS KARACHI KUALA LUMPUR
CAPE TOWN IBADAN NAIROBI ACCRA

© *Oxford University Press* 1958

Printed in Great Britain
The Whitefriars Press Ltd., London and Tonbridge

FOREWORD

The Whidden Lectures were established in 1954 by E. C. Fox, B.A., LL.D., of Toronto, the senior member of the Board of Governors, to honour the memory of the late Reverend Howard P. Whidden, D.D., LL.D., D.C.L., F.R.S.C., 1871–1952, Chancellor of McMaster University from 1923 to 1941. The purpose of the lectures is to bring to the University scholars who will help students to cross the barriers existing among the academic departments of a modern University. The lectures are not restricted as to general theme.

Dr. Whidden was a member of a family resident in Antigonish, N.S., since 1761, after earlier settlement in New England in 1700. Born in Nova Scotia, he was educated at Acadia University, McMaster University, and the University of Chicago, and subsequently served as the minister of Baptist churches in Ontario, Manitoba and Ohio. From 1913 to 1923 he was President of Brandon College in Manitoba, then affiliated with McMaster University, and served in the House of Commons in Ottawa from 1917 to 1921 as the Union Government member for Brandon. Assuming responsibility as chief executive officer at McMaster in 1923, he was responsible for negotiations and actions leading to the transfer of the institution to Hamilton in 1930, from Toronto where it had been established in 1887. He is

FOREWORD

remembered as a man of striking appearance, unusual dignity, effective leadership, ready tolerance, deep Christian conviction, and broad educational outlook. Chiefly to him the University owes what amounted to its second founding.

The third series of lectures on the foundation was delivered in January 1958 by Ronald Syme, M.A., F.B.A., Camden Professor of Ancient History in the University of Oxford, on *Colonial Élites: Rome, Spain and the Americas*, a topic of current as well as historical interest because of the continuing effects in the Americas of a pattern of settlement and of power that was not dissimilar to that in the Mediterranean area earlier.

Born in New Zealand, Ronald Syme has combined an academic career at Oxford with excursions into political service and sustained contributions to the world of scholarship. Fellow of Brasenose College, formerly Fellow of Trinity College, and sometime Professor of Classical Philology at the University of Istanbul, he served with H.M. Legation in Belgrade, 1940–1, and with H.M. Embassy in Ankara, 1941–2. He has been President of the Society for the Promotion of Roman Studies (1948–52), President of the International Federation of Classical Studies (1951–4), Secretary-General of the International Council for Philosophy and Humanistic Studies (1952), and is a member of the German Archaeological Institute, of the Royal Danish Academy of Letters and Sciences, of the Lund Society of Letters, and of the Bavarian Academy. His publications include *The Roman Revolution* (1939), *Tacitus*

FOREWORD

(1958), articles in learned journals, and certain chapters in the *Cambridge Ancient History*.

His visit to this University was his first introduction to Canada and Canadian institutions. He addressed an audience whose thought and ways have been strongly influenced, whether by way of reaction or imitation, by the theories and practices of the strong men who led in settlement and exploitation distantly or immediately south of the Canadian border in the sixteenth to eighteenth centuries.

THE PRESIDENT'S OFFICE G. P. GILMOUR
McMASTER UNIVERSITY
May 1958

CONTENTS

	Foreword by G. P. Gilmour	v
I.	The Spanish Romans	1
II.	Spanish America	24
III.	English America	44

I. The Spanish Romans

It is no small honour to be invited to deliver the Whidden Lectures so soon after their inception. The series led off with various problems of race and nationality in the contemporary world, first South Africa, then India. We now go back two thousand years and hold discourse on Spain in the time of the Romans. Ancient history, it will be said, and what relevance can that have in this late season?

A further question, however, could be put. When shall modern history be supposed to take its beginning? There is a ready answer: it starts with the Renaissance and with the discovery of the New World. That is a familiar and defensible notion. But, it could also be argued, on the present and changing perspective, the modern age does not truly begin before the eighteenth century. On that count, a study of the colonial establishments of the Spaniards and of the English before they separated from the mother-countries can suitably be adduced for comparison with an epoch of Roman history.

The world has seen three empires notable for their wide extent and long duration—Rome, Spain and England. The Romans extended their domination to the extremities of the known world: it reached from

Spain and Scotland as far as the River Euphrates, the desert of Arabia and the cataract of the Nile. Spain held a large portion of the Americas all the way from California down to Patagonia. The English sent their colonists across the ocean, they ruled India, their name and language and institutions obtain at the furthest end of the world, in the Antipodes.

Empires suggest the inevitable theme of decline and fall. Rome itself furnishes the classic example in the title and volumes of the great English historian Edward Gibbon. The debate on the fall of the Roman Empire is one that continues to this day. Gibbon put the emphasis on two main causes: the invasions of the northern barbarians and internal subversion by a new and vigorous religion, issuing from Judaea. But there are many other factors. In the first place perhaps sheer distance, the strain on communications and the enormous extent of the Empire; and from time to time scholars have been impelled to invoke various other causes, such as economic stagnation, the burden of bureaucracy, the failure to develop scientific inventions—or indeed ingrained conceit and an excessive worship of tradition. In our day the ingenious polymath Arnold J. Toynbee comes out with a general theory to explain the decline of all civilizations. He adduces the growth of what he calls an 'internal proletariat,' carrying with it a universal religion which permeates and destroys a civilization. Whatever be thought of that, there is a question which Arnold J. Toynbee and others might well have asked themselves: not the causes for the decay or termination of empires, but rather how and why is it that some of them managed to last as long as they did.

What was it that through the centuries held together the vast empire of the Romans? In the first instance, no doubt, the structure of the imperial system and the principles of government. That will not take one far enough. A structure can turn out to be only a façade. What is behind it? The principles of government may appear firm, enlightened and sagacious. Are they always put into effect? The thing that matters is not the structure, and not the principles, but the men, those who are selected to carry the burden of administration: if you like, the oligarchy of government.

Rome, republican and imperial alike, exhibits the remarkable phenomenon of a governing class which changes steadily through the ages. That was due, not to any theory or doctrine, but to the pressure of facts, acknowledged by a conquering aristocracy—and also by the Caesars and their ministers. As Rome spread her domination over Italy in the time of the Republic, she brought into her ambit the best men from the Italian communities. Similarly, when the Republic gives way to the Empire, the new system that emerges does not hold down or exclude the nations and cities that had come under Rome's dominion. In the past the Romans had been generous with grants of the citizenship; and they now admit to their governing order the leading members of the provincial aristocracies, drawn not only from the West but, after no long interval, from the eastern lands. Hence there is a long and steady process

of development in what might properly be called an
'open society' or indeed an 'expanding society'.

Those terms are recent indeed, all too familiar, and in
danger of being vulgarized. They have been employed
by writers whose concern is modern history exclusively,
or the philosophy of history. What Rome achieved tends
to be ignored.[1] The reason is plain (but the omission
none the less deplorable and criminal). The Romans
themselves failed to produce any lengthy or searching
disquisitions. The best and almost the only exposition
of how the governing class was transformed through the
ages is a brief summary, casually preserved. The historian Tacitus, for his own good purposes, decided to
reproduce (and improve) an oration of Claudius
Caesar on that subject.[2]

There emerges therefore a theme of no small pertinence. The strength and vitality of an empire is frequently due to the new aristocracy from the periphery.
It may be instructive in different ages and civilizations
to study the origin, composition and behaviour of provincial or colonial élites. Various problems arise. Are
these provincials descended from colonists of earlier
days, do they return to their country of origin, do they
stay there and impose their claims? Or, alternatively,
are they of alien origin but having fully assimilated the
language and habits of the dominant civilization? or
again, are they of mixed origin? And finally, touching
the rise and fall of empires, stands the peremptory
question about the colonial notables: do they secede
from the mother country, and, if so, for what reasons?

Does the home government endeavour to conciliate and keep them? Could secession perhaps have been averted by the exercise of one of the prime political virtues, I mean forbearance and patience?

In this matter Roman Spain presents a contrast to the Spanish domination in the two Americas and also to the Thirteen Colonies of the English in North America. Let me therefore turn to Spain in order to explain what role was played in the Roman Empire by the new élite. Most of the Roman provinces were acquired while the constitution of Rome was still that of a republic. The Empire takes its beginning with Caesar Augustus, who in the year 31 B.C., by winning the Battle of Actium, put an end to the strife for power and terminated the civil wars. By his victory Augustus rescued Rome, Italy and the West from Marcus Antonius, his rival, and also from the foreign woman, the Queen of Egypt—Cleopatra. He rescued Rome, and that action was fervently acclaimed at the time, and has been much admired subsequently. In the course of years, under that system which Augustus founded, it was not possible to protect Rome from an invasion of a different kind—a peaceful invasion from the provinces of the Roman West.

One can distinguish in the first century of the Roman Empire three rich, populous, and dynamic regions. First of all, in Italy itself, the Cisalpina, and in the Cisalpina the zone that extended between the River Po and the Alps, namely Transpadana. Secondly, the old Roman province in the south of France, Gallia

COLONIAL ÉLITES

Narbonensis. And finally, Spain. Not the whole of the Peninsula, to be sure, but the prosperous and civilized tracts along the eastern coast, and in the valley of the Ebro; and also, on the south-west beyond the Straits of Gibraltar, the small territory which the Romans called Baetica (roughly equivalent to the valley of the River Baetis, the Guadalquivir). In terms of medieval or modern history, these regions of wealth and energy could be described as, first of all Lombardy and Venetia, secondly Provence and Languedoc, thirdly Catalonia and Andalusia. It will not be necessary to expatiate on the role played in European history and civilization by those six names.

During the early period of the Roman Empire these countries are prominent in literature and also in government. Even before the Republic ended there was a poet of original genius from northern Italy beyond the River Po, Catullus from Verona; and, not long after Catullus, come the shining glories of Augustan Rome, Virgil for verse, Livy for prose (from Mantua and from Patavium). When they were born their country still had the status of a Roman province, not yet a part of Italy. Later, in the course of the first century A.D., the palm for literary achievement seems to go to the western provinces outside Italy, and especially to Spain. One need mention only the Seneca family, the poet Martial, the professor and literary critic Quintilian.

The repute of Spain in polite letters is matched by its prominence in government. Under the early Caesars the working of the imperial system comes to depend strongly on men from the western provinces. They serve as officers in the army and as financial agents of the emperors. Next, they can enter the upper order of society (the Roman Senate), they rise to the highest rank, namely by holding the office of consul; and furthermore, after the consulate, they govern the great military provinces of the Empire, for example Britain, the German commands on the Rhine, or the province of Syria.

The Roman Republic as a system and constitution seemed devised to ensure the division of powers. The Empire by contrast means centralized government, regular routine—and even 'planning'. The Emperors need friends, allies and helpers to perform the diverse functions; they require a bureaucracy. If there is a bureaucracy, who will comprise it? Not the old families but the alert and ambitious men, ready to serve the Caesars and the Empire. Now a bureaucracy can be invaded, permeated and captured by groups of individuals. That is precisely what happened at Rome in the course of the first century of our era. It is not altogether fanciful to detect something like what has been acclaimed in the modern world, namely, the so-called Managerial Revolution, which brings a wonderful opportunity to the educated and efficient classes.

Let me give an example by names and persons. Seneca to all posterity is known as 'Seneca the Philosopher'. He was something more than that, something different, as the historian Tacitus is careful to demonstrate. The copious author of ethical treatises was also a

COLONIAL ÉLITES

Minister of State, comparable to those great cardinals to be discovered in French and Spanish history three or four hundred years ago. When in the year 54 of our era the Emperor Claudius died (an accelerated death) the succession went, as was planned, to Nero. Nero was aged only seventeen. Who had charge of policy and government? The eloquent and diplomatic Seneca is disclosed. Seneca was a Roman from Spain, from the south-west, from the old city of Corduba. Seneca did not stand alone, his strongest ally was the Commander of the Praetorian Guard, a certain Afranius Burrus. Now this man comes from a small town in the south of France, Vasio (the modern Vaison, about twenty-five miles north-east of Avignon).

For half a dozen years Rome and the Empire were managed by the conjoint efforts of two men issuing from the western provinces. It was too early for any of this type to take over the power entirely, and wear the purple of the Caesars. But that was to happen before long. In the year 97 a weak emperor, Nerva, unequal to a desperate political crisis, was compelled to take a strong man as his associate in the power. He chose one of the army commanders. This was Trajan, the son of a consular senator from Spain; his family derives from Italica, which is not far from the modern city of Seville. Thus begins the dynasty of the Antonine emperors, Spanish and Narbonensian by origin, under whom the Roman world enjoyed the high summer of its felicity—and its autumnal season. To explain how it was that the new men from the western provinces went so far and advanced so quickly in the Roman Empire it is expedient to look a long way back into the history of the past.

It is suitable that Spain should have produced the first extraneous emperor. Spain could be termed ' the oldest dominion '. How and why was it acquired by the Romans? The historian Edward Gibbon in a striking phrase proclaims that Spain, ' by a very singular fatality was the Peru and Mexico of the old world '. The Romans exploited the precious metals, but it was not for gold or for silver that they went originally to Spain. Their arrival had a strategic or accidental reason. The date is 218 B.C., at the beginning of the second of those great wars fought for the mastery of the western Mediterranean between the two imperial republics, Rome and Carthage. Hannibal for his invasion of Italy used Spain as a base, the Romans therefore landed in Spain to cut off his supplies. Once there, they found themselves involved and engaged in constant warfare, and so the armies remained. After the termination of the Second Punic War the Romans set up two provincial commands in the Peninsula, as geography dictated. The one corresponded roughly to the modern Catalonia, the other, in the south-west, to Andalusia: in Roman terms, the Two Spains, Hither and Further. Long wars ensued with the fierce Celtiberian tribes of the central plateau; and the mountainous north-west of Spain, extending in a wide sweep all the way from the north of Portugal to the Pyrenees, was not subjugated by the Romans until the time of Caesar Augustus, precisely in the year 19 B.C. That is to say, two whole centuries.

What had been going on in that long period? We happen to know very little. Most of what stands on record is warfare, either campaigns against the native tribesmen or the local repercussion of Roman civil wars in the last epoch of the Republic. Otherwise only odd scraps of information are available about normal and peaceful developments. One has to serve them up and (let it be confessed) supplement them with a fair measure of guesswork. To that end, one may be tempted to invoke analogy or parallels, some of them to be drawn from the colonization and exploitation of the Americas by the Spaniards and by the English.

First of all, immigration. It was both military and civilian. The Roman army properly so-called was confined to Roman citizens, but the Romans also used men of the Latin status (an inferior type of citizenship) and levies from the communities of Italy which lay outside the Roman State in the period before 91 B.C. It will be recalled that the unification of Italy came at a late date in history. Many of these soldiers, Roman citizens or not, would wish to stay behind in the rich lands of high civilization in Spain rather than return to cultivate the thin soil or rough slopes of some Appennine valley. Similarly, traders would be attracted to exploit the resources of the peninsula: the mines and the fisheries, the vine and the olive. Labour was cheap (slave or native); there will have been war booty available;

land-grabbing will not have been eschewed. The profits of war and of trade went into real estate, and in the course of those two centuries something of a propertied aristocracy had time to grow up. Refugees had also come to Spain from Italy as a result of various disturbances beginning with the revolt of the Italian allies in the year 91 B.C.

Moreover, in this period town settlements formed, of various types. Before Scipio left Spain in the year 206 he established a settlement at Italica for soldiers from his army. Then, in the year 171, there happens to be registered an isolated incident which may not perhaps have looked so isolated to contemporaries.[3] Four thousand men sent a petition to the Roman Senate. These were persons lacking a proper civil status, for they were the sons of Roman soldiers and native women in Spain. The Senate had to do something about these people, and therefore a colony of the Latin right was created for them at a place called Carteia, not very far from the Straits of Gibraltar. Then, about twenty years later, the Romans established a colony at Corduba. The colony was inhabited not only by the Romans but by select individuals from among the natives.[4] In later history this is what very often happened when the Romans created a colony of veteran soldiers in the provinces: they incorporated in the foundation some of the better sort of the natives.[5]

Race was no barrier, neither was religion. Intermarriage (it can be assumed) did not run counter to any of the traditions or practices of Mediterranean civilization. In course of time the Roman citizenship came to be granted with great generosity even to Spanish auxiliary soldiers (*en bloc* sometimes).[6] It was a normal reward for prominent individuals in the Spanish towns who had loyally served the proconsuls of the Roman Republic.[7] Furthermore, a number of the native towns themselves were promoted in status by the grant of Latin rights. That meant that the magistrates became Roman citizens. Hence a simple and automatic device for rewarding and attaching the right people, namely, the local magnates.

Through the combined working of these various factors a high culture had already come to maturity in Spain before the fall of the Roman Republic, before the planned military colonization which Caesar and Caesar Augustus carried out.[8] It was a product of commerce and the cities—and city life was an ancient phenomenon in certain parts. There were already many flourishing urban centres in the Two Spains. Notable among them are Corduba in the far south-west, Tarraco and Carthago Nova on the eastern coast. Corduba could show poets among its citizens. There was a wealthy and energetic town aristocracy, the ex-trading class now owners of large estates. Among its members one would be entitled to postulate Seneca's father, born and educated at Corduba.

What was the relationship between the local notables and the Roman government? Now Spain is some distance from Italy, and in fact the Romans established themselves in the Peninsula long before they were in possession of the land road from Italy to Spain. Apart from military emergencies, the Roman government under the Republic can hardly be said ever to have had a Spanish policy. Did the Spanish Romans therefore feel that they had been neglected? Or did they resent being subject to the proconsuls? A mild measure of social or political discontent can be a useful stimulus to ambition. Further, was any new spirit or local patriotism developing, hence a tendency towards secession?

That, unfortunately, cannot quite be established.[9] Before many years had passed the Roman provinces were swept into the whirlpool of Roman civil war. Active individuals espoused various causes in turn and duly ended on the right side, the *clientela* of Pompeius passing to Caesar and Caesar Augustus. Hence they are concerned in the foundation of the centralized government under which they prosper by gliding into good positions. They migrate to the capital in permanence; they purchase mansions at Rome, villas and estates in the fashionable vicinity; they invade the high strata of society; they contract marriage alliances with Italian families, and even with the old Roman aristocracy; and also, and naturally, with similar groups of rising families from other provinces, such as Narbonensis. They began as clients of the Caesars and they end by supplanting them.

Such in outline is the class of the new Romans, alert, energetic and highly successful. But who, more precisely, are these Spanish Romans? How far are they of immigrant stock, how far do they descend from civilized natives, how far are they a product of 'superior miscegenation'?. Can the components be discovered and assessed? Perhaps, perhaps not. There is a further question: how much did it matter, anyhow?

Various criteria can be adduced. The Peninsula, although compact in shape, is far from a unit, as the study of its geography tells, and as its war-torn history reveals. The territories to which there had been the greatest migration were, as one would expect, the eastern coast and the far south-west. The bleak central plateau offered no temptation. Furthermore, the status of a man's town may be an indication. That is to say, is it a Roman colony or is it in origin a native town? But here inquiry must pause and hesitate because (as has been seen) even in Roman colonies in the provinces there can be ex-natives as well as persons who possessed the Roman citizenship by birth.

There is, however, another method, a new technique, namely, the investigation of family nomenclature. If you will permit me a brief excursus, I will tell you how it can be exploited. The family name (*gentilicium*) of Seneca is 'Annaeus'. That is not an old Roman name at all. It points to central Italy, i.e., the odds are that the ancestors of Seneca were not Roman citizens. Nor were they Spanish natives. Secondly, the family name of the Emperor Trajan is 'Ulpius'. This is not an old Roman name either. It is probably indigenous somewhere in central or eastern Italy, deriving from one of the Illyrian dialects.[10]

An important consequence follows. The ancestors of Ulpii, Annaei and other families of substance and repute in the region of Baetica will be sought among the early settlers: small people, Italian soldiers or traders, whatever genealogical claims or fancies were later on parade. If they took native women for wives, that was long ago; the evidence was faint or discreetly covered up and not easily verifiable to posterity.[11]

Another part of Spain can yield a contrast, the old Celtiberian country. Martial was born at Bilbilis, Quintilian at Calagurris. Neither town had begun as a settlement of Roman citizens. Martial was a 'Valerius', Quintilian a 'Fabius'. Those names are common in Spain, of a type that often reveals personal grants of the Roman franchise made by proconsuls in the days of the Republic. If race and extraction be held to matter, there are diversities to be registered—and possibly put to some use.

From time to time scholars or men of letters, publicists or patriots, have been tempted to discover typically Spanish features in certain of the Spanish Romans. Pomp and splendour of rhetoric seem to characterize the writings of Seneca and his nephew Lucan. For that reason and for others (among them the Stoic doctrines and attitude), Spaniards have been exceedingly proud of these authors. But the style and thought of Seneca and of Lucan can have nothing whatsoever to do with the climate and geography of Spain or the local origin of the family. They reflect contemporary fashions in Rome of the Caesars.

Again, some have pointed to the personalities of Trajan or of Hadrian as exemplifying influences of race

COLONIAL ÉLITES

or soil or climate. A German professor, writing in the *Cambridge Ancient History*, exults on that theme.[12] 'Hadrian's strength,' he says, ' was born of the mingling in him of old-Italian and Iberian and perhaps African-Semitic blood; the ocean, the plain, now luxuriant now sun-stricken, and the sluggish river at the south-western edge of the Empire left their mark on his family and childhood.' It will suffice to observe that, whereas Hadrian's family came from Italica (its ultimate origin being from the region of Picenum in Italy), Hadrian himself was born at the capital of Empire, where his father was a senator.[13]

Or again, a more temperate and subtle writer, an Englishman expounding the history of Spanish literature. While sceptical about certain current estimates of Seneca and Lucan, he claims that he can perceive Aragonese features in both Quintilian and in Martial.[14] Those two authors had their home towns in the country subsequently called Aragon, it is true; and a ready contrast is available between Aragon and Andalusia in medieval and modern history. What can or should thence be deduced about the style and personality of Roman writers?

Martial, it is true, alludes often and affectionately to the mountains and rivers near his native Bilbilis; yet Quintilian's town would be an enigma but for a casual mention preserved by a chronicler in late antiquity. The provenance of Quintilian could no more be divined from his writings than can those writings be invoked to confirm and illuminate it.

Social history may be a better clue than geography. Martial and Quintilian derive from a newer stratum than the plantation magnates of the far south-west. Their families could not compete in wealth, antiquity and prestige.[15]

Speculation is slippery or fallacious. To return to the question of alien or blended antecedents. The Romans evince no sort of preoccupation with racial purity. How could they? Many nations are prone to embellish and exalt their birth and origins but the legend of the foundation of Rome is anything but flattering—bastards and brigands. The components of the Roman People were mixed from the outset, Latin, Sabine and Etruscan; and the Italy which the Republic subjugated and incorporated was a mosaic of languages—Oscan, Etruscan, Celtic, Illyrian, Venetic, Ligurian.

An aggressive and tenacious power, the Republic needed men and resources as it expanded. That expansion was not merely territorial—peoples and cities were brought into the ambit of a common citizenship. If a man was good enough to fight for Rome, he was good enough to be a citizen. Such at least is the maxim enounced by Cicero when speaking in defence of a man from Gades, in Spain. The Romans, he adds, have never worried where anybody comes from, and therefore they have commonly preferred 'virtus' to pedigree.[16]

It is personal quality that counts, not race or origin. The provincials from the western lands embody many types of merit, and not least the reassuring fact that they conform to certain of the cherished ideals of Roman tradition, notably that simple and old-fashioned way of life which (in the pages of Roman poets or moralists) is so often deemed to have deserted the metropolis, being only discoverable in the Sabine country, or in the towns of northern Italy and the West.

A new nation is not new in all respects. It is an observable phenomenon in other ages that colonists preserve habits of life or speech no longer current at home; and the Spanish language in fact goes back to a form of Latin more archaic than does French. The Spanish Romans (it might seem) parade and exploit their loyalty to the old Roman traditions. On the other hand, their resplendent success proves them eager, ambitious and innovatory.

The qualities and employments that ensured their advancement can be discovered or divined. For the Spanish magnates the best evidence is supplied by items about the family of Seneca—father, mother and brothers. There is not much else. Perhaps it is legitimate to fill out the picture with some details about a similar aristocracy, that of Gallia Narbonensis (where, it may be observed, most of the notables are indigenous by origin, not of immigrant stock).[17] For the Narbonensians there is available an explicit document, nothing less than the biography of Julius Agricola, consul and governor of Britain, composed by his son-in-law Cornelius Tacitus as his first essay in the evolution that was to take him from oratory to the writing of history. Agricola was born at the ancient and illustrious *colonia* of Forum Julii, of native extraction ultimately, as his name ' Julius ' indicates. His father was the first senator of the family; both grandfathers had been finance agents of the Caesars. The *Agricola* of Tacitus expounds the behaviour and ideals of the new imperial aristocracy now triumphant.

An essential and much-praised virtue in the Roman tradition was frugality and a horror of conspicuous expenditure. It is duly advertised by new men, both Italian and provincial—and the term ' provincialis parsimonia ' was in currency. To be parsimonious with effect and success, you need to have quite a lot of money. The provincial parvenus appear to be adequately endowed. Land was the basis of social prestige and political influence, but not everybody could turn his estates to profit. Provincials, however, were skilful in introducing new agricultural methods; and some wrote textbooks.[18] The wealth of Seneca incurred envy and blame. Not all of it had accrued from Nero's bounty or the sale of patronage. Seneca purchased vineyards near Rome for an enormous price, yet was soon able to sell to advantage.[19] They might also be adepts at commerce and finance. Seneca himself went in for banking operations.[20] The great minister was a practical man. He could have acquired a wife from some resplendent family of the old Roman aristocracy. Instead he married the daughter of Pompeius Paullinus, the official in charge of the food supply of the capital (a Narbonensian from Arelate).[21]

Mere wealth did not lead to the summit of Roman

society. In default of birth, talent was needed: military capacity or the gift of speech. At the beginning of Nero's reign, the commander on the Lower Rhine is disclosed as the brother-in-law of Seneca; his successor in that post came from the same town of Narbonensis (Vasio) as did Afranius Burrus, the Prefect of the Guard. Not that these were great generals: safe steady men were the requisite. The working of patronage is convincingly attested.[22]

Seneca was one of the greatest orators of his day. Eloquence was the crown of Roman education, and provincials paid it a zealous tribute. Education, however, does not stop with style and words. It may attract the young along dangerous paths of thought. The Romans had a deep distrust of doctrines. The parent of Seneca, a pattern of ' antiquus rigor ', was bitterly hostile to philosophical speculation: he tried to impede his wife's efforts at self-improvement, and he was perturbed by certain youthful aberrations in his son.[23] And Agricola's mother intervened, with quiet admonition, when the young man embraced the study of philosophy ' with more ardour than is suitable in a Roman and a senator '.

Agricola was thus rescued for the service of the Roman State. In his career he maintained careful regard for discretion and subordination; he was active and efficient, never ostentatious; he avoided political attitudes and kept clear of entanglement with imprudent and doctrinaire critics of autocracy. In this manner, as Tacitus explains, Agricola served Rome and the

Empire; he demonstrated that it was possible for there to be great men even under evil rulers.

Agricola (as the historian is unobtrusively suggesting) stands as a precursor to Trajan. With the accession of that emperor is revealed the predominance of the new Romans of the West. Integrity, industry, and good sense have prevailed, so it should seem. A doubt might arise about success stories, ancient or modern. The new men, as presented in the literary evidence, embody the steady honest virtues of the ancient and exemplary Romans. Success demands other qualities. As can be observed in political life (and even in the life of academic communities) the ostensible plain man is not always simple-minded. Many of the characters with whom we are dealing were alert and refined, smooth and astute.

They have a good report. The reason of it may be obvious and natural. Not merely the use and abuse of conventional phraseology: most of the writers who supply the information belong themselves to the rising classes. Among them will plausibly be enrolled the historian Tacitus: surely not (as some have fancied) a descendant of the patrician Cornelii but rather a Roman of the West, from some town in the province of Narbonensis.[24]

If that be so, Tacitus, a consul before he became a historian, is a phenomenon parallel to Trajan, his coeval. Energy, ambition and opportunism brought the provincial élite to the conquest of the metropolis. Let us not depreciate these men or suspect their virtue and

COLONIAL ÉLITES

their value. The process is at the same time the triumph of the educated class in the Roman Empire, and that, I venture to say, is a subject not unsuitable to be commemorated when one is speaking at a University.

NOTES

1 As in the book of K. R. Popper, *The Open Society and its Enemies* I (1945). There was less excuse for a historian nourished on the ancient classics. See the pertinent criticism of J. F. Leddy, ' Toynbee and the History of Rome ', *The Phoenix*, XI (1947), 4 ff.

2 *Annals*, XI. 24, cf. the copy of the original on the bronze tablet at Lyon (Dessau, *Inscriptiones Latinae Selectae*, 212).

3. Livy, XLIII. 3.

4 Strabo, III, p. 141. Despite this precise testimony, however, the origin and status of Corduba is not without perplexities.

5 As is known for Colonia Claudia (Cologne), cf. Tacitus, *Histories* IV. 65, and may be inferred for other *coloniae* such as Forum Julii (Fréjus).

6 Thus the cavalrymen rewarded for service against the Italian insurgents in 89 B.C. (Dessau, *Inscr. Lat. Sel.* 8888).

7 The prime example is Cornelius Balbus of Punic Gades.

8 Strabo the geographer, writing in the middle years of Augustus' reign, affirms that the natives in the south-west had become completely Roman (III, p. 151). As elsewhere, his testimony may reflect conditions that prevailed a little earlier than the time of writing.

9 Despite the episode of Sertorius—or incidents like the plot against a Roman governor in 48 B.C. (*Bellum Alexandrinum*, 48 ff.).

10 Cognate, that is, with ' lupus ', ' wolf ', ' vuk ', as Jacob Grimm divined long ago. Observe also the Dasumii of Corduba, whose name is Messapian, from south-eastern Italy.

11 The Greek historian Cassius Dio made the baseless assertion that Trajan was an ' Iberian ' (LXVIII. 4).

12 W. Weber in *Cambridge Ancient History*, XI (1936), 325.

13 *Historia Augusta, Hadr.*, 1. 3.

14. G. Brenan, *The Literature of the Spanish People* (1953), 2: ' We are on safer ground when we speak of the Aragonese character of Quintilian and Martial.' In the former is extolled a ' dry, sober, gentle common sense ', while Martial had ' the Spanish eye for vivid detail ', also ' a Spanish spontaneity ', and further, ' the Spanish philosophy of man '.

15 That contrast is in fact recognized by Brenan (op. cit., 5).

16 *Pro Balbo*, 51.

THE SPANISH ROMANS

17 Observe the striking contribution from Nemausus and Vienna: both cities began as the capitals of native tribes.

18 Thus Agricola's father (an authority on viticulture) and Columella of Gades (who had several Italian estates).

19 Pliny, *Nat. Hist.* XIV. 51. As that author notes, Seneca was ' minime mirator inanium '.

20 Thereby damaging his repute with posterity. Cassius Dio alleges that Seneca provoked the great rebellion in Britain by calling in his loans suddenly (LXII. 2).

21 The man to whom Seneca dedicated the treatise *De brevitate vitae*.
22 cf. R. Syme, *The Roman Revolution* (1939), 503.
23 Seneca, *Ad Helviam matrem*, 17; *Epistulae*, 108. 22 (vegetarianism).
24 cf. R. Syme, *Tacitus* (1958), Ch. XLV.

II. Spanish America

Romans from cities in the two Spains, immigrant or mixed stock, were able to assert parity at the metropolis and ultimately to enforce predominance. Their success was furthered by various factors. Spain in certain of its regions offered an ancient and congenial Mediterranean civilization, with cheap land and labour and resources for enrichment through agriculture, mining and commerce. Towns rose and prospered, more by a natural growth than by any policy of the Roman government; and, if the local magnates developed some of the vigorous independent qualities of a frontier zone, their ambitions or grievances did not issue in rebellion and secession from the Imperial Republic. Before that could happen, a new system of government emerged, which the provincials supported, infiltrated and captured.

It was a long process, two centuries from Scipio to Caesar Augustus and another to the accession of Trajan; and, despite gaps and guesswork, it becomes intelligible. Now the Spanish Empire in the Americas endured for three centuries before it split up. Spanish America is a challenge to investigation, in the manifold features of resemblance or contrast.

It is not an easy theme. Apart from the alluring narrations of exploration and conquest, the Spanish

Empire has not been studied with proper assiduity in the English-speaking countries. Many universities (and not the lowest in prestige and pretensions) were long neglectful or still remain largely indifferent.

The reasons are in no way mysterious. The sharpest censure should perhaps be visited on the preoccupation with national, domestic or parochial history—to many no doubt a theme of inspiration, zeal and reward, yet all too often narrowing and deadening. Prejudice has also operated, of various and convergent types. The power of Spain was predominant in Europe for the greater part of the sixteenth century, and the English resistance to Spanish imperialism, culminating in the defeat of the Armada, will be honourably recalled. Hostility and rivalry were enhanced by economic interest, for the Spanish government tried to keep a monopoly of all commerce with the New World—most distasteful to traders, slave-dealers or pirates of other nationalities. And lastly, requiring no exemplification, the irreconcilable strife of two religions. Hence the 'Black Legend' of the Spanish Empire—tyranny and bigotry, greed and cruelty.

The most telling evidence about the maltreatment of natives, so it happens, was brought up by humane and conscientious Spaniards—to be seized upon with alacrity by enemies of Spain and of the Catholic Church. Something deserves to be said on the other side. In the early period, at least, sincere attempts were made to treat the Indians in a tolerable fashion. They were not merely regarded as raw material for conversion; it was intended that they should be educated as well. The record of the first English colonists in North America, notably those in New England who paraded high principles of religion and morality, shows hardly a trace of laudable aspirations towards native welfare, let alone any programme of action.[1]

The Inquisition is not a thing easy to be named without horror and detestation. It will be observed, however, that the operations of the Holy Office were not directed against Indians but only against heretics; heresy was not a frequent failing among the Spanish colonists; and the Inquisition does not seem to have done much to inhibit the growth of free inquiry among the educated classes.[2] Similarly, the government was more liberal in practice than in theory, being baffled by incompetence, hypocrisy or human frailty. Its rigorous enactments are known: how far were they executed? For example, the strictest of royal regulations attempted to control the export of books to the New World and prevent the dissemination of noxious and even of frivolous literature (to the latter class belonged those romances of chivalry to which Charles V himself was so passionately addicted). Certain facts only recently disinterred are a counsel to scepticism about laws and principles. The archives at Seville have disclosed bills of lading for all sorts of ostensibly dubious books, duly countersigned by royal officials.[3]

And finally there is this to be said for the Spanish Empire. There flourished in its cities a brilliant European civilization which fostered literature and the arts.

SPANISH AMERICA

When men pass judgment on the past, they tend to award the palm to high culture, which has normally (and indeed exclusively) been the product of cities and of minorities. Athens is praised, and Rome—while the slaves and serfs and the voiceless earth-coloured rustics are conveniently forgotten.

The civilization of Spanish America still acknowledges the conditions that presided at its birth. The exploration and conquest of the New World came in an appropriate season, with a miraculous concordance of determining factors. It was in 1492 that Columbus received his commission from Ferdinand and Isabella. The two crowns of Aragon and Castile had just been united, and this same year saw the Reconquest completed when the last relic of the Moorish power, the Kingdom of Granada, was annexed. Spain became strong, confident and aggressive.

The enterprises across the ocean are a direct continuation both of the Reconquest and of the campaigns against the infidel in North Africa. Nor was the most solemn of religious sanctions absent. The Catholic monarchs had a Bull from the Pope in 1493 (a Spaniard, it happened, Alexander VI), and, soon after, the whole of the western world was delimited between two nations, Spain and Portugal. Not only a crusade. The Spaniards, ever conscious of imperial Rome (and haunted perhaps by the fame of their Trajan), were impelled by a deep sense of mission to conquer and also to govern.

COLONIAL ÉLITES

Glory lured them, heroic attitudes and the thirst for adventure.[4] The Conquistadores were transported into strange realms that resembled the ancient and legendary East. Theirs was a fortune like that of the Greeks who saw Memphis and hundred-gated Thebes and the gardens of Babylon. The classic myths of Argonauts and Amazons came alive again, and later fables seemed bare truth. Novels of romance were the favourite reading of an age that lacked the detective novel or science fiction. Their influence is detected in the words of Bernal Díaz del Castillo describing the Vale of Mexico:

> When we beheld the number of populous towns on the water and firm ground, and that broad causeway running straight level to the city, we could compare it to nothing but the enchanted scenes we had read of in *Amadis of Gaul*, from the great towers and temples and other edifices of lime and stones which seemed to rise out of the water. To many of us it appeared doubtful whether we were asleep or awake.[5]

The Conquistadores in their normal behaviour were anything but visionaries; and it would be a singular imprudence to fancy that men crossed the wide ocean under the stern dictates of religion or wantonly hazarded their lives from sheer exhilaration. Gold and precious stones and enormous enrichment drew them. They imagined that their sails were set to the Indies and, beyond, to Cathay or Japan. As Heredia puts it (himself a Spaniard of Cuba),

> ils allaient conquérir le fabuleux métal
> que Cipango mûrit dans ses mines lointaines.

Mexico or Peru, there was less of gold than they expected. Avidly seized and ferociously disputed, Montezuma's treasure and the hoards of the Incas were quickly scattered. Looking back on their epic adventures, the survivors could not help being sad and querulous. Thus Bernal Díaz, who ended his days as a municipal magistrate in Guatemala, writing the narrative of the Conquest in his eighties. Others, however, if disappointed of gold, won broad estates and a lordly way of life. That had not been their lot and fortune in their Spanish homeland, otherwise they would never have gone to the Indies.

Portugal began the work of oceanic exploration, and it is no surprise that harbours on the Atlantic furnished shipmasters and sailors for the Spanish ventures. Seville and Cadiz are duly in evidence; and one small port, Palos, supplied the three captains of Columbus on his first voyage. The Conquistadores, however, come from inland regions of the Peninsula. Their local distribution is instructive.[6] Castile, not Aragon, took the lead in the conquest and exploitation of the New World. Therefore hardly anybody from Catalonia (despite the alert and venturesome character of the Catalans). By contrast, Estremadura is prominent, namely, the western-central region of Spain towards the Portuguese frontier. It is a hard land, bare and rugged, sun-smitten in summer, chill in winter. Cortés came from Medellin, the Pizarro brothers from Trujillo. Other towns in this country produced Balboa, Pedro de Alvarado and de Soto. Later emigration in the course of the sixteenth century

COLONIAL ÉLITES

conforms to the original pattern. Most of the people come from a tract that extends from Andalusia northwards towards Burgos and east to Toledo and Madrid. There are also some Basques, but Galicia (though maritime) is not strongly represented, nor, on the other flank of Spain, Catalonia, Valencia and Murcia.

Like true Spaniards, the original conquerors were disposed to exalt their quality and pedigree. Who was not a noble in Spain? It appears that few members of the high aristocracy went to the Indies, and few from the great military families—they had active and profitable employment already. The class and type of the adventurers can be divined—casual items preserved or an easy and normal assumption. They were sons of the impoverished local gentry or small-town bourgeoisie out of work (and not wanting work); and some of lower status still. Cortés had some benefits of education—two years as a law student at the University of Salamanca. He emigrated to the Indies to better his fortunes. Reputable scandal registers an escapade with a lady in Cuba before the expedition to Mexico; and, scarcely landed on the mainland, by subtle arts he enlisted for the Spaniards the indispensable aid of a woman (a captive but born a princess) whom they called Doña Marina. The quality of Cortés is evident in his generalship, his diplomacy—and in the despatches he sent to Charles V. Very different from the conqueror of Peru. Pizarro was brutish and repellent, the illegitimate son of a butcher, and totally illiterate.

The Conquistadores behaved as might have been

expected from their antecedents and their desperate ambitions, exasperated by the hardships they had to endure in mountain, forest and desert. One recalls the arduous and daring march of Cortés from the coast of Mexico to the plateau, or Pizarro's men in Peru, going up into the high country ten and even twelve thousand feet above sea-level—much higher perhaps than they could have known (for the barometer had not yet been invented); and before long Chile was penetrated, the Andes were crossed, the River Amazon navigated to its mouth.

In their behaviour the Conquerors were reckless, ruthless, like men intoxicated—'ivres d'un rêve héroique et brutal' (as the poet Heredia puts it). Heroism or ferocity, they surpassed all adventurers of the other nations—and they had unparalleled opportunities for greed and licence. Would the energetic English, who before long tried to infringe the Spanish monopoly, have comported themselves much more soberly if they had Mexico for their prey and portion? Restraint and stability will not safely be postulated of men like the pirate and slave-trader Sir John Hawkins.

The Spaniards burst for the first time into realms of gold and romance. They found rich civilizations that had evolved a long way, complex and highly organized, resembling the empires of the ancient East. They were peculiar. Mexico lacked beasts of burden, wheeled traffic and iron tools. Yet not everything was exotic. Montezuma's empire, the product of a conquering people, the Aztecs, was an intelligible structure, precariously resting on a confederation of cities and tribes (and hence, as Cortés saw, easily to be subverted). A king, an aristocratic class, and a priesthood, cities with temples and palaces, that too was familiar. A question arises, in the alluring field of the historical 'might have been'. Cortés gained control and dominance over Montezuma, inducing him to swear homage to the Christian Emperor. Would it have been possible to preserve the fabric and system of Montezuma's kingdom as a fief of the Spanish crown, the Spaniards in control, permeating but not destroying?

A vain question, no doubt. Too many factors militated on the other side. Yet, as it happened, the social structure suited the needs and appetites of the invaders. Both in Mexico and in Peru an upper class had developed. The chroniclers speak of daughters of the nobility, taller and fairer than the common sort, of refined manners and gracious in demeanour.[7] Concubinage was a predictable consequence. And marriage sometimes followed, if a man were not led away by ambition for a bride from Spain.[8] Two Spanish noblemen married daughters of Montezuma, Isabel and Leonora; while Doña Elvira, daughter of one of the four rulers of Tlaxcala, entered an eminent Spanish family; and when the famous Doña Marina was discarded by Cortés, she passed to a Spanish captain—the daughter of this match inherited half a province to rule. These instances, one is tempted to say, make the Pocahontas story look rather silly. As for Peru, one of the Inca's daughters bore a son to a Spanish nobleman, but not in wedlock.

SPANISH AMERICA

The fruit of this marriage was the Inca Garcilaso de la Vega, an educated and intelligent man, who wrote about the antiquities of his own people. So much for the upper order in society. As few Spanish women of any class came with the first waves of invaders and immigrants, intermarriage took place in all ranks of the army with the native women.

There were no barriers, no inhibitions.[9] Why should there have been? Various reasons can be adduced. The Spaniards were heirs of that old Mediterranean civilization that knew no colour bar.[10] How indeed could it have? Dark pigmentation is frequent in the Mediterranean—and indeed it is recorded that some of the natives of the New World were paler in complexion than a number of Castilian Spaniards. Spain itself before the Romans went there had been a blend of races, not only Iberian and Celtic. Subsequently, after the fall of the Roman Empire, Spain was invaded by various tribes, first the Germans, then the Moors. The Moors were mixed, some Arabs among them, some Berbers from North Africa. There was also an immigration of Jews. Spaniards themselves may have been uncomfortably aware of all that the Moors and the Jews had contributed to the civilization and especially the economic development of their own country.

Further and finally, the doctrine of the Church of Rome, preaching human brotherhood and also accepting any kind of marriage, as better than none at all. Hence in the New World a considerable admixture of native blood from the very beginning. The process has gone on steadily, more visible in some regions than in others. The Spaniards indeed have lacked the peculiar aptitude, the positive genius of the Portuguese. Compare the blend of strains in present-day Brazil—a fantastic amalgam.

So far the Conquerors, in their provenance, conduct and ambitions. They were well on the way to carve out independent principalities for themselves, but the Spanish government was on its guard. The new territories were dominions of the Spanish Crown—in fact kingdoms. Hence viceroys were soon appointed to govern them; and from Spain a strict control was exercised. For politics and administration by the body called the Council of the Indies; for trade and commerce by the House of Trade. The Spanish government kept careful watch over emigration. For example, no foreigners or heretics were allowed to go; unmarried men were discouraged; a censorship tried to regulate the export of printed matter; and a monopoly of trade with the West was conferred on the merchants of Cadiz and Seville.

In the New World government was firmly and centrally organized.[11] Spain itself had only just come to unity. The kings and their ministers could remember the dangers which regionalism and individualism presented in Spain itself. They were suspicious (and with reason) of the energetic individuals who had gone to seize wealth and power beyond the seas. It is not surprising that before long there even arose from the ambitions and greed of the Spaniards in Peru monstrous civil wars. As for Mexico, though Cortés the Conqueror was given the title of Marquis of the Valley of Oaxaca, he was not allowed to become Viceroy.

It was over the native question that the Spanish government came most sharply into conflict with the Conquerors and the early colonists. What was the proper status of the Indians? What could the Spaniards be permitted to do in virtue of the right of conquest—or was there such a right? God's viceregent on earth gave dominion to the Spaniards, but had also enjoined a responsibility on them especially and above all the nations of Europe. Now, at this time, the Spaniards were most fanatically devoted to legal theory and to legal forms.[12] The natives were subjects of the Spanish Crown. Was it therefore right to enslave them?

In the first epoch in Mexico promising beginnings were made in the sphere of native welfare and education. There was even a college established in Mexico City—the College of Santa Cruz, for young men of the upper class, where they learned Latin. You might be surprised to discover that there were also schools for girls. Furthermore, an attempt was made to introduce local government in native communities on the model of Spanish towns.[13]

These experiments came to nought, for predictable reasons. The conquerors and colonists had not come to till the land themselves: they had come to better their condition and live like Spanish gentlemen. They needed a labour force. The practice grew up of entrusting a number of native villages to some Spaniard. He was supposed to protect and cherish the Indians. In return they were expected dutifully to provide help and labour for him. This is what is known as the Encomienda system. As may well be imagined, such a system would naturally develop into exploitation and slavery. There was, however, a deep disquiet felt about Encomiendas by the Spanish government and by the Church. There were men who felt the prick of conscience. One of them was the Dominican friar Las Casas. As a result of his tireless efforts the Spanish government in the year 1542 promulgated what was called the New Laws.[14] But this noble attempt was of no avail. It caused anger and turmoil in Mexico and a revolution in Peru. It was quickly found impossible to enforce the laws: the colonists needed land and working men.

Hence the system which obtains in the New World is one of large estates exploited by native labour. That did not preclude or impede the growth of towns. The new local nobility would not be content to spend all its time on country estates and in fortified manor houses. Let us recall that before the Spaniards there had been great urban agglomerations in Mexico. The Spaniards proceeded to build cities either where the old native towns had been or on new sites. It was indeed a tradition of the Spaniards to establish cities. This feature may owe something to their Roman memories. More, perhaps, to the realities of the reconquest of Spain from the Moors: the border territories called for strong places, not vulnerable villages. Cortés himself, no sooner landed in

Mexico, established a municipality at Vera Cruz.[15] Other generals followed his example, eager for the renown of 'pobladores'. Furthermore, the Spanish government took a serious view of town planning. It issued instructions to show how cities should be built, with a church, a municipal palace and a central plaza.

This city civilization of Spanish America has its definite characteristics visible to our own day. It bears a strong clerical imprint. There were many cathedrals and churches, monasteries and nunneries—and much of the land was in the possession of the Church or mortgaged to the Church. Literature and various branches of the arts flourished, and erudition was valued. Let it never be forgotten that in the year 1551 two universities were established in the New World—one at Mexico and the other at Lima. Theology had its strong claims, but the study of the Greek and Latin classics was assiduously pursued, and not in translation only. Classical texts were edited, there were commentaries and learned disquisitions. One's curiosity cannot fail to be whetted by the fact that in the year 1645 there was printed in Mexico a book on Roman imperial history entitled *El Político Tiberio César*.[16] I regret that I have not yet set eyes on that volume.

That these cities abode in splendour and luxury we have evidence from contemporaries. One of the most remarkable witnesses is a certain Thomas Gage, the English friar who visited Mexico in the year 1626, and many years later, having been converted to Protestantism, wrote a vivid and lurid account.[17] Further, from a

COLONIAL ÉLITES

Spanish source we have in the *Annals of Potosí* a picture of life at high altitudes in a mining city: it was vigorous and unrestrained—drink and duels and gambling and even small civil wars.[18] As for the conduct of the clergy, and especially of the higher clergy, I think it would be discreet to draw a veil over that.

Such was the civilization of Spanish America—a transplantation of Renaissance Europe in its brilliance and turbulence, and not without features that recalled the Mediterranean cities of earlier ages, Greek or Arab. A question must now be put: how did the colonial aristocracy stand in the eyes of the mother country? Tension was not slow to emerge between the colonials and Spaniards from Spain—and it might be enhanced by the superior wealth of the former class, and by their pretensions (which could not always be supported by purity of blood and descent). According to the testimony of Thomas Gage, Creoles and Spaniards detested each other.

Not many of the Creoles (it appears) were tempted to return to Spain in permanence. It could not be easy for them to make their way to positions of eminence in Church and State—and an education could be got in the colonies. These new Spaniards fail to make any notable contribution to the literature of the homeland, apart from the playwright Alarcón.

On the other hand, staying where they were, they found their ambitions repressed. The Spanish government was highly suspicious of the descendants of the

SPANISH AMERICA

Conquerors: few were permitted to rise high. The statistics are eloquent.[19] By the year 1813 only four viceroys were native born (and these were sons of officials from Spain). It was easier perhaps for a foreigner to make his way—observe the O'Higgins who became Viceroy of Peru in 1796. The Church was less forbidding—in the same period about a hundred bishops out of seven hundred were Creoles. Yet even so, in 1808 all the bishoprics in Mexico except one were held by Spaniards from Spain.

The Creoles grew discontented. Yet it was a long time before the split occurred. As the eighteenth century advanced, the Spanish government itself was becoming less rigid. The influence of the Bourbon dynasty and of the French enlightenment is invoked, and perhaps overpraised—for English ideas and advisers should not be left out. As for the New World, the government was relaxing its deadening grip on trade, and the colonies were prospering. It is indeed affirmed that in the decade 1778–88 the commerce of the colonies had multiplied sevenfold.[20] Furthermore, new ideas were spreading through the dissemination of European books.

Then came the heady example of two revolutions, the American and the French. And accident supervened. Spain being occupied by Napoleon, the colonists had an excuse and pretext to break loose. And there was the opportunity of foreign aid, the English not reluctant to take a hand in subverting the empire of an old rival that became a temporary ally in the struggle against despotism in Europe.

The new doctrines had exasperated the discontent of ambitious Creoles. And, as with some of the gentry of the English colonies in their contest with the English government, classical education had a part to play. A notorious and engaging anecdote tells how, on an August day in the year 1808, Bolívar along with his friend and mentor Símon Rodríguez climbed up the Mons Sacer outside Rome, the place to which the plebeians had seceded.[21] Bolívar was impelled to declaim on the history of Rome. In the course of that history, he said, all things had been witnessed—but nothing had been done by the Romans for the cause of human liberty. The solution, he affirmed, must come from the New World. The ardent Bolívar therefore took a solemn oath to destroy the Spanish Empire.

Roman history can teach other lessons: patience, distrust of theory and a preference for slow developments. It happens to be a Spanish poet, Magi Morera, who produced a useful definition of Utopia, namely, something that does not occur in the history of the Roman People.[22]

The liberty to which Bolívar aspired was only for a minority. The revolution in Spanish America was the work of a few educated and ambitious individuals. A large part of the population (it seems) was really loyal to Spain and the monarchy, reluctant to break away. There ensued a bitter civil war, and in some territories, especially in Venezuela, untold horrors and atrocities. The Spaniards of Spanish America secured liberation from the home government, but that act brought no

SPANISH AMERICA

change in the social structure. No truly democratic movement was started, such as came after no long interval in the English colonies in northern America. Nor was any unity possible, only fragmentation, from the earliest days of the rebellion. Hence that multitude of republics which we observe today and can barely name or remember. A multitude, yet they have had their common lineaments. Since their liberation the republics of Latin America have furnished a lavish chronicle of oligarchy and of tyranny.

Spain itself, among the nations of Europe in the modern age, is a kind of disappointment. In the sixteenth century Spain excelled not only in arms but in the arts, not only in military science but in law and government. Predominant in Europe, Charles V and Philip II held a vast empire beyond the seas, with a steady revenue of precious metals. But the gold of the Indies was spent in vain, or operated detrimentally. The government pursued perverse economic policies, trade and industry languished. Despotism, officialdom and the discouragement of intellectual effort induced torpor, enhancing certain defects in the Spanish psychology.[23]

Coming first in the field, the Spaniards in their dynamic epoch seized the countries of greatest wealth in the New World; and by a singular fatality it happened that some of them settled in high plateaux that bore a resemblance to their own homeland. In New England the English found a familiar landscape and climate, but it will be recalled that, in the middle of the sixteenth century, it was Virginia and the colonies in the West Indies that constituted the most valuable and populous of their possessions.

The Spanish and English colonies afford certain obvious contrasts; and speculation about their divergent fortunes in the sequel is an engaging topic of speculation. Toynbee, developing his theory of the greater challenge to human effort presented by 'hard' countries than by 'soft', can point to the success of New England.[24] Now, to take extremes, what greater contrast in the way of life than Boston matched with Mexico City or Lima in the colonial period? Yet it would be legitimate to observe that the configuration of Spanish America, with its high mountains and arid plains, could also on that principle have been an exacting challenge.

In spite of the handicaps of geography and of distance, Spain was able to hold her wide dominions for three centuries and set upon them indelibly the stamp of her language, thought and institutions. That achievement deserves more honour than it has commonly earned—and a more searching investigation.

NOTES

1 For an eloquent (and sometimes intemperate) defence of Spanish imperialism see S. de Madariaga, *The Rise of the Spanish American Empire* (1947); *The Fall of the Spanish American Empire* (1948).

2 Other things retarded them more, such as traditionalism and the cult of *belles lettres*.

3 cf. the investigations of Irving A. Leonard, conveniently summarized and elegantly set forth in *Books for the Brave* (1949).

4 For the Conquest and also for the social life of the Spanish colonies see the excellent book of W. L. Schurz, *This New World* (1954), with its alert detail and lively portrayal.

5 Quoted from the translation of M. Keating (New York, 1927).

6 For the facts, cf. V. A. Neasham, 'Spanish Emigration to the New World, 1492–1592', *Hispano-American Historical Review*, XIX (1939), 147 ff.

7 W. L. Schurz, op. cit., 277 f.

8 cf. the detailed study of C. E. Marshall, 'The Birth of the Mestizo in New Spain', *Hisp. Am. Hist. Rev.*, XIX (1939), 161 ff.

9 As W. L. Schurz dryly remarks, 'the customary pattern of their relationship . . . was uncomplicated by any efforts at moralizing or rationalizing on either side', op. cit., 299.

10 For some observations about the colour-bar cf. S. de Madariaga, *The Fall of the Spanish American Empire* (1948), 89 ff.

11 For the administration see C. H. Haring, *The Spanish Empire in America* (1947).

12 As most conspicuously and ridiculously shown by the *requerimiento* read out to natives by the self-righteous invaders when seizing a new territory.

13 C. Gibson, 'The Transformation of the Indian Community in New Spain, 1500–1810', *Journal of World History II* (1955), 581 ff.

14 For this theme of high debate see J. H. Parry, *The Spanish Theory of Empire in the Sixteenth Century* (1940); L. Hanke, *The Struggle for Justice in the Conquest of America* (1952).

15 That action was, it is true, an artful device to evade the control of the Governor of Cuba and establish an independent link with the Spanish monarchy.

16 T. B. Jones, 'The Classics in Colonial Hispanic America', *Transactions of the American Philological Association*, LXX (1939), 43. The book presumably dealt with statecraft and Macchiavellianism: it finds no entry under 'Tacito en Hispanoamerica' in the work of F. Sanmarti Boncompte, *Tacito en España* (1951).

17 T. Gage, *The English American. A new Survey of the West Indies*, edited by A. P. Newton, 1928. The first edition appeared in 1648.

18 cf. the extracts cited and exploited by S. de Madariaga, op. cit., 24 ff.

19 C. H. Haring, op. cit., 209 ff.

20 C. H. Haring, op. cit., 342.

21 Cited and discussed by S. de Madariaga, *The Rise of the Spanish Empire* (1947), xii.

22 Cited by J. Bainville, *Lectures* (1937), 39.

23 The decline of Spain is the modern parallel to the Roman Empire —and would repay intensive study.

24 Not that he is altogether convincing. For sharp criticism see P. Geyl, *Debates with Historians* (1955), 149 ff.

III. English America

Like Spain itself, the Spanish establishments in the Americas seem not to have been wholly successful. Against them stands for contrast English America. There the political and social structure helped. We think with due gratitude of the vigour and vitality of their institutions—while, at the same time, recalling that even after the American Revolution the system cannot quite be called democratic. Furthermore, as contributing to the success of the Thirteen Colonies, when they broke loose, is the fact that they had not been harshly treated by the British government, whatever grievances were adduced and exploited. The Spanish government, keeping a tight hand on trade, also curbed the local aristocracies in the Spanish colonies; their leading men were not allowed to rise to high positions in Church and State. By contrast, in English America colonials could in time aspire to colonial governorships.

No doubt, it might be said that the Thirteen Colonies had been neglected rather than oppressed by the British Government. Sometimes indeed they were regarded as a nuisance. These colonies were able to prosper, however, and to survive—and in their survival there is one factor that not everybody has been able to acknowledge cheerfully and gratefully—they were protected from the

French and the Spanish by the British Navy. Let it be added that they would not have been able to bring to success their Revolution without help from the enemies of England.

Let us turn now to the origin of the Thirteen Colonies. The English establishments in the New World came a century later than those of the Spaniards—hence there were obvious differences. For example, different aspects of European civilization were represented by the Spaniards and by the English. On the one hand, the Renaissance, a largely literary culture; on the other, the Reformation, with the spirit of inquiry, and, indeed, of criticism and rebellion. The Spaniards, arriving first, annexed what seemed the richest territories, especially the countries of ancient civilization in Mexico and Peru. With these possessions, however, they acquired a native problem. The English in America were more fortunate, for the natives were not numerous; they were primitive and scattered. In fact, despite several raids and massacres, not much of a problem. It is true that some had thoughts of converting and civilizing the Indians (the Bible was translated at an early date), but, on the whole, our New Englanders or Virginians do not seem to have worried very much. They lacked the zeal and application of the Spanish priests, who were prepared to learn native languages and undertake long and arduous journeys. Neglect, enmity or extirpation, the English record in the treatment of Indians is not altogether a happy one.

Something has been said about the contrast between

COLONIAL ÉLITES

the English and Spanish establishments in the New World. The antithesis is far from complete. We think, in the first instance, of the colonists in New England and in Virginia. Let it be observed, however, that in the seventeenth century the English settled in a wide zone from New England southwards, including the West Indies. This is to say, in the South and in the Islands, the settlements offer some resemblance to Spanish and tropical America. Moreover, certain periods of the seventeenth century show much emigration from England to the West Indies. Out of some 60,000 people who left England in the years between 1620 and 1640, it appears that about half went to the West Indian islands.[1] Once again, therefore, dealing with English America after Rome, Spain and Spanish America, I am faced, and indeed bewildered, by a large and formidable subject. Think, for example, of the diversity of the settlements, all the long way from New England down to Georgia. It is therefore expedient to restrict and concentrate. Studying the origin, growth and behaviour of the colonial élites in the English America, I shall try to lay the emphasis on Virginia and New England.

Legend or popular history presents a conveniently simplified picture of these two regions. Virginia, we all know, was aristocratic and wealthy; cavaliers abounded there, and Royalists, with a most elegant and gracious way of living. New England, on the other hand, was Puritan. The citizens were grave and orderly in their ways, virtuously poor and salubriously democratic.

More detail, it would appear, is desirable. If we turn to New England, and especially to Massachusetts, it is clear that these colonies began in opposition and almost in secession, and the results are notable for centuries thereafter. The Puritans left England to escape persecution (less rigorous, perhaps, than they imagined or proclaimed), they wished to set up in another country their own little republics, there to develop their own conception of divine worship and civil government. Freedom of worship they insisted on, but it was only for themselves. There is another story—the story, for example, of how they persecuted people who did not agree with them, and especially the Quakers. It was not toleration they wanted, but liberty for themselves, and domination. This is to say, not democracy in any sense, but rather a religiously guided oligarchy, a theocracy.[2]

The religious motive in the emigration is evident. It was not the only thing. It was not only strict and practising Puritans that crossed the seas. Many went precisely to improve their economic condition. In England in the years from 1620 to 1640 there had been an economic crisis with much unemployment in agriculture and in small industries. That makes one inquire more closely into the class and the social structure of the colonists in New England. Some of the names preserved suggest the lower gentry or the middle classes. We also discover that there were a number of artisans and labourers; and the local extraction of the emigrants can be established from various types of historical record, not to omit the appellation of villages in New England or the names that a man can read today when he contemplates the gravestones in their cemeteries.

One of the features that is notable, and has not been neglected subsequently by the proud sons of New England, is the extent to which the educated class was represented among the emigrants.[3] In New England, about the year 1646, the total population can hardly have exceeded 25,000. In this total there were no fewer than 130 university graduates, which, even on modern and, perhaps, inflated estimates in a number of countries, is a considerable proportion. And it is significant that most of these were graduates of the University of Cambridge, with quite a large bunch coming from a single college, namely, Emmanuel. The emigration as a whole exhibits strong local characteristics—Cambridge rather than Oxford, East Anglia rather than Southern and Central England.

How did these model colonies develop? It had been intended by the leaders of the different projects that they should establish in New England a kind of federation of agricultural villages under the permanent and strict control of the Puritan clerics. Villages, because there was no room for large estates, and there were not enough natives available who could be made to work. Nor was there a single staple product like tobacco, that could be exploited by slave labour, as happened in the South. If the soil was poor, there was timber and fish. The New Englanders had to take to the sea. Maritime trade flourished, and by the end of the seventeenth

ENGLISH AMERICA

century we discover emerging that remarkable economic phenomenon, and highly satisfactory, the triangular trade: namely, rum made in New England, exported to West Africa in exchange for slaves who were transported to the British West Indies to work in the sugar plantations from which region molasses was exported to New England, where it was converted into rum.[4] And so the process continued steadily, profitably, and not blamed even by the clergy. These successful economic operations produced a large number of shipowners and traders. Hence in the maritime cities of New England and, notably, Boston there arose a commercial oligarchy.

Commerce and town life, as in other ages, meant a subversion of traditional ideas. Hence enlightenment or rebellion. Nobody will neglect the role played by the different cities of the Thirteen Colonies in the American Revolution. By 1776 cities such as Boston and (less fervent for Revolution) Philadelphia and New York probably had a dynamic importance in the British Empire equalled, after London, only by Edinburgh and Bristol.

Furthermore, in the process of time, the control usurped by the Puritan clergy tended to break down. The ministers themselves were educated men. They acknowledged the supremacy of reason, they discoursed not a little upon it. They went in for erudition. They saw the value of the natural sciences. Hence the rigidity of the old system relaxed. It might be said that the logical end of the educated clergy in New England is what in effect happened later on—they changed from Puritanism to Unitarianism.

The predominance of the clerical profession declined. Eloquent and ambitious young men, instead of becoming preachers and theologians, decided that it was a more useful career to go in for the law. Moreover, the prestige of the clergy in the last decade of the seventeenth century was impaired by those remarkable trials for witchcraft at Salem in 1692. As a result of the belief in magic and sorcery of certain of the higher clergy in New England, of the persecution of witches or believed witches, with the death penalty for some twenty or thirty people, opposition arose, notably among the merchant class. Among the enemies of the great Puritan theologians (such as Cotton Mather) are found two merchants, Thomas Brattle and Robert Calef. The second of these two men wrote a damaging parody of the work of Cotton Mather. He called his pamphlet *More Wonders of the Invisible World*.[5]

When the eighteenth century dawns in New England, the governing class is already being transformed. It becomes a society of merchants and lawyers, secular in outlook, competitive and indeed contentious in behaviour.

Meanwhile a different form of life had been developing in the South and especially in Virginia.[6] In the early years there certainly arrived from England a few members of the highest nobility. But it would appear, on scrutiny, that most of them died or went away. Instead, the lower gentry or their younger sons, or various adventurers who came to improve their condition and set themselves up as English country gentlemen. They profited from trade, there was plenty of land available, and labour of one sort or another could be obtained. In the first instance, and here I refer to the 'black' or suppressed history of Virginia—convicts transported from England. Some of them genuine criminals, to be sure. But perhaps, it can be urged in extenuation, some of them were simply enterprising people or victims of political change. There was also the system of indentured labour whereby poor men sold themselves into slavery for a period of about seven years with the hope and prospect of liberty thereafter, and the acquirement of 50 or 100 acres of land.[7]

These are the facts that must be borne in mind when one is confronted with any impressive or ancient genealogy of Virginian families. A decisive period of social change and advancement seems to belong in the years after 1680, when the price of tobacco began to rise sharply, and, with the price of tobacco, the influx of slaves to work in the plantations. Early in the eighteenth century we can discover the lineaments of the traditional Virginian aristocracy, exemplified by the names Byrd, Carter, Randolph, Lee.

These were families that held large estates. They were now able to build splendid mansions and were concentrating their influence through intermarriage. To take two examples. The first John Carter appears to have been a distressed Royalist, a gentleman but not of any high significance. The second, who was born in the year 1663, distinguished himself by acquiring 300,000 acres and no fewer than 1,000 slaves. The first William Byrd was a trader. His son, William Byrd II, born in the year 1674, was a man of taste and fashion who dabbled in literature, went to London, and was seen in the best circles.

In the course of time smaller men rise and prosper. For example, famous among the Fathers of the Revolution, the excellent Thomas Jefferson, who married a wealthy widow. Hence, as the peak of contrast, we see the country gentlemen of Virginia aspiring to an English way of life, and the town aristocracy of Boston, merchants and shipowners. In all ages of history it is desirable to get away from generalizations and study individuals and families. The present argument is concentrated on the higher ranks of society, neglecting the lower, because most is known about them—and, indeed, because they have the greatest freedom of action. But in passing let it be remembered that the history of the upper order in the Thirteen Colonies is not the whole history of English America.

I have alluded to the contrasts of social life between North and South. They come out in a vigorous and healthy rivalry among American historians in the modern age according to their origins or political beliefs. By a singular chance, in the interests of historical accuracy or plausibility, these writers are quite willing to subvert and destroy the sacred legend either of the South or of the North—but they do not usually destroy both at the same time.

There are various subjects of discord and controversy which can be seized upon. Imagine the satisfaction of a virtuous New Englander when he discovers that the ancestors of some armorial family of Virginia began in poverty and obscurity. On the other hand, the defenders of the South will point out that New England in its early epoch did not quite stand for political and religious liberty. Again, education, where New England clearly has the primacy. Harvard College was founded in 1636. Naturally Virginia cannot touch that! In the same year was established the famous Boston Latin School, where the young could not get anywhere until they had first studied the Latin language for seven years on end. This was a remarkable school which produced its heroes or martyrs of education. Notable among these was the patriarch Ezechiel Cheever, who, I believe, died still in harness at the age of ninety-two.[8]

The disputants also adduce the state of general education in the North or the South. They appeal to statistics of the libraries owned by colonial worthies—New England has the famous Cotton Mather, but erudite though this man was, he was excelled by the Virginian William Byrd II, who could boast a library of 3,600 volumes. Appeal is made to schools or universities, education or private libraries, by both sides, perhaps because neither can point to literary production which could rival the nations of Europe. However, various sorts of obscure literary practitioners are brought up and exhibited in competition.[9]

Nor were scientific attainments neglected. Scholars

COLONIAL ÉLITES

have carefully gone into the details preserved about members of the Royal Society of London before the year 1776. Here, of course, New England is allowed to triumph. One estimate produces fifteen members of the Royal Society before that date, nine of whom are from New England, with only three from Virginia.[10]

Perhaps, however, the contrast is most clearly seen not in comparisons between society and civilization in New England and in the South, but in the relation of each region to the mother country. For that is one of the themes of this course of lectures. What classes of people went back to the mother country and why? Did they stay there, and with what success?

Various reasons brought colonial Americans back to England. Religion, education, family ties or business interests, each and all were of influence. Let me select and segregate two periods only.[11] First, the Civil War and the Commonwealth. The Puritans founded colonies in New England, and they remained there, with momentous results. But, ought we not to ask, did all of them intend to go out to the wilderness in permanence? Were they not, perhaps, only retiring for a time across the seas until conditions in England took a turn for the better, until Archbishop Laud should die or the domination of the Anglican bishops be abolished?

The chance came for their return with the Civil War and with the Commonwealth. Here are some statistics. Of the Harvard class of 1642—not a very numerous class, it is true—seven of the nine went to England. In

Cromwell's army, New England provided about six colonels, and there were about eight Members of Parliament. Above all, the talents and tastes of the New England men found them a suitable employment in the Civil War and under the Commonwealth as Army chaplains. For example, Hugh Peter, an active and eloquent person, who, like others since, found that journalism and the ministry are not incompatible. In fact, he served as a war correspondent. It appears, however, that he had made himself objectionable in other ways as well. At the Restoration, though he was not among those who had voted for the condemnation of an English king, he was linked with the Regicides and, like them, executed.

A different fate was reserved for one of the earliest Harvard graduates, George Downing. He inaugurated his return as Scoutmaster-General in Cromwell's Army in Scotland. An interesting title, when one considers that, at this time, it designated the agent in charge of espionage. He subsequently became a Member of Parliament, and he was employed on diplomatic missions in Europe—on one of them he met the redoubtable Cardinal Mazarin with whom he interceded on behalf of persecuted Protestants in the Valais. It is not recorded that his efforts had any result. His career, however, suffered no impediment, and he survived the end of the Commonwealth by good fortune. At that juncture he was out of England and out of danger, being the English representative with the Dutch government. Charles II made him a knight, and then a baronet.

COLONIAL ÉLITES

This is the man who ended, suitably enough, by giving his name to a street in London, precisely Downing Street. It is clear that his career had exhibited certain necessary qualities of a diplomat, among them a notable versatility.

The second period which witnesses the return of men from the English colonies is the thirty years before 1776. Many travellers are attested in England in this period. Not merely tourists or business men. Young men went for their education to schools or to the universities, among them many more from the South than from the North.[12] Why might this be? Presumably because the Southern landowners, the new gentry, felt themselves in a closer relation of affinity to England; and it might be added that the educational facilities in the South could not compete with those of the North. Towards 1750, one can detect a great increase in the number of persons seeking a higher education or professional training in England.[13] At Oxford, at Cambridge, at the Inns of Court in London, at the Medical School at Edinburgh. Before the Revolution, there had been at Edinburgh about a hundred American students. Oxford and Cambridge account for about seventy each. Of each seventy, almost a half came precisely from Virginia.

If there was this influx into the old country for the purposes of education, why not that further stage which often follows on the higher education—participation in public life? Ought not some of these men to have sought election to Parliament? Especially, would we not expect to find some Virginians among the Members of Parliament because of their wealth, their social gifts and their Anglicanism (not that faith was in fact very deep or fervent in colonial Virginia)? It appears not to have been so. We are, therefore, impelled to ask what prevented them from entering Parliament? We can look about for reasons, discovering them as best we may. It is a fair supposition that men were attached to their ancestral estates in Virginia. It was not at all easy to set up as a country gentleman in England. Virginians were wealthy landowners, not averse from display and expenditure, but they may not have had the resources of ready cash needed for residence in England and for the financing of elections. Furthermore, as emerges from the accounts of some travellers, various aspects of life in London were distasteful to men from the New World. They were repelled by the extreme contrasts between wealth and poverty in London, by the political corruption and the immorality, by the dirt, the smoke and the fog.[14]

It is true that in this period there were 'Americans', in one sense of the term, among the Members of Parliament. I refer to planters from the West Indies. These formed a group—a kind of 'sugar group'. It has been alleged that in the year 1777 they were about forty in number. That is enormous, and not to be believed. Once again, it is expedient to turn to details and facts about individuals and families.[15] Inquiry shows that this 'sugar lobby' totalled only thirteen, although in passing it may be said that no fewer than seven were from Jamaica. Of those seven, six belonged to one and the same family group, being connected with William Beckford, the largest landowner in the island. The men of the Thirteen Colonies at this time were highly suspicious of the 'sugar aristocracy' of the West Indies, perhaps unduly. They themselves, in the year 1761, had not a single representative in the English Parliament. It can, however, be pointed out that between the years 1763 and 1783 there were five North Americans in Parliament, all of them from the northern or central States.[16] Notable among them is a merchant from New York by the name of Henry Kruger, who sat for Bristol along with the famous and eloquent Edmund Burke. Just before the fatal year of 1776, relations between the colonists of North America and the home country seemed to be growing much closer. It was a time of great prosperity in America. But that prosperity had not brought contentment.

The population was, according to historians, probably between two and two and one-half millions by 1776. In this period, a resplendent future could have been foretold for English America—but, presumably, a future under the English Crown. May I, at this point, quote from a letter addressed by the philosopher Hume to young Edward Gibbon in the year 1767? Gibbon (he was then aged thirty) was thinking of composing history and he proposed to write in the French language. Hume, in reply, objected: 'Let the French, therefore, triumph in the present diffusion of their tongue. Our solid and increasing establishments in America, where we need less dread the inundation of barbarians, promise a superior stability and duration to the English language '.[17]

The prospects seemed solid and resplendent. None the less, the breach came. Hence the occasion of a great debate among historians, a debate which cannot here be more than indicated, though I would wish to affirm (on my brief and superficial acquaintance with this theme) that American historians in the last fifty years have shown a remarkable fairness in dealing with the difference between the colonies and the mother country. They have also shown unbelievable alacrity in subverting the conventional and sacred legend which is the heroic past of their own country, the great epoch of the Revolution.

Their revolution succeeded. Therefore, on one view of history, it is a ' good thing ', and there is nothing more to be said about it. Let us, however, in passing emphasize the hazards which the Thirteen Colonies confronted, the extreme unlikelihood of their staying united until they secured their uncontested liberty. Observe, for example, the distance of the colonies one from another, the long line of them strung out along the Atlantic seaboard from Maine down to Georgia, the long sea passage, the absence of adequate roads by land. Observe, further, how extremely heterogeneous they were: it seems a miracle that Massachusetts and Virginia could have been induced to co-operate. Again, the role of accident and of individuals in their military enterprises. It was John Adams, of Boston, who insisted that leadership of the rebel forces go to a Virginian by the name of George Washington. And finally, among other things, could they have hoped to succeed without foreign aid? Before the year 1776 is out the able and astute Benjamin Franklin, a man of enormous prestige, had already arrived at Versailles, soliciting men and arms for the insurgents.

It is a temptation to ask, was the breach then inevitable? It can, of course, be said (and it is said by some) that in truth the revolution had already happened in the previous two generations, for the Americans and the English had already grown so far apart.[18] Yet it was not the English way to press for a quick solution of political problems, and, to revert to the general topic of these lectures, it was not the Roman way either; or again, it was not always the Spanish. Antonio de Mendoza, the first Viceroy of New Spain, pronounced an excellent maxim. He said: ' Do little and do that slowly '.[19]

Such, surely, are the counsels which some of us would have recommended to both sides in the years after the Seven Years' War! Unfortunately, both sides had taken up attitudes and put themselves into positions from which there could be no retreat. Many of the upper order in the American colonies clearly were driven further than they intended. They appealed to principles, which trapped them and compelled them to take action. We will register their imprudent toleration of mob violence in cities such as Boston; we will note the combination of high ideals and financial interest; and we will not omit the contagious influence of demagogues, not only in Boston, where the notorious Sam Adams raved and ranted, but even among the Virginians. Patrick Henry, it is reported, exclaimed (possibly more than once) ' Give me liberty or give me death! ' This is a striking utterance. Sober reflection should ask whether Patrick Henry, as a practical politician, contemplated extinction, or, when declaiming about liberty, he meant all men and all classes of society. This ejaculation is surely something not wholly English, not, perhaps, truly American. Is it not a histrionic and Latin-American attitude?

More plausible and reasonable at first sight might appear the claim that there should be no taxation without representation. Is it certain, however, that the Americans wanted representation? Could it, in effect, have been given to them? It is true that some people played with this idea. Franklin was for it for a time. The English economist, Adam Smith, said that it might be ' a new and dazzling object of ambition ' to colonial leaders, but Edmund Burke ridiculed the notion at some length.[20]

The factors of time and place and distance confirm the negative view. It might take five weeks (sometimes much more) for the voyage either way. The expense of public life was a deterrent to parsimonious New England and ostensibly opulent Virginia alike. And how was access to membership of Parliament achieved? Not by virtue and merit, confidently facing the free suffrages

COLONIAL ÉLITES

of a free people. Patronage operated—the King, the political managers, the various factions.

The structure of the English Parliament was anything but representative. It would have been necessary to remodel the constitution. That is to say, tamper with the palladium of English liberties. That would have been repellent, not only to the Englishman but also to the better sort in colonial America, who were loyal to the political traditions of Great Britain. English habits and attitudes tend to be exaggerated beyond the seas, and not least in America. It would have been ' unthinkable ' to change the British constitution.

Otherwise it might amuse a philosophical mind (a phrase of the eighteenth century can here be employed) to inquire what would have happened if certain of the American worthies had been transported across the Atlantic there to refresh and reinvigorate the governing aristocracy of Great Britain. One of the paradoxes of history is the long survival of senior statesmen. The year 1826 witnessed the death of two of the heroes of the American Revolution—John Adams and Thomas Jefferson. What might not have been the role and value of those individuals in English public life? Jefferson, repenting, perhaps, of his addiction to French ideas, Adams, clearly a useful character (very different from his cousin Sam), a man of sound principles, hostile to change and eminently trustworthy. John Adams ought to have got on very well with Lord North.[21]

Or what of the great Benjamin Franklin? It happens to stand in the books that he ended his long and varied career in the year 1790. Suppose his vigour and vitality had preserved him for three or four years longer. We can then see him duly elevated for public service to the peerage as Lord Franklin, that inventor and practical philosopher, a plain man, but far from simple. His energy unabated, Franklin would no doubt have reverted to journalism, but in a superior capacity, as one of the lords of the daily press. And with what aims and what policy? Surely he would have preached imperial free trade and imperial preferences; and he would roundly denounce the excesses of the French Revolution, for these things were un-English. I am, of course, going back to the topic with which these lectures began. I am thinking of Rome. You may suspect that I am coming very close to Canada.

The theme could be carried much further, if one toys with the fancy of prominent men from the colonies returning to public life in England. Their activities might not in themselves provoke disturbance or a revolution. Yet there might have ensued some bigger and better civil war in the British Empire, with a battle of Gettysburg decided along the escarpment of Niagara.

Speculation of this kind you might find empty and vain. I utter it only because there is this to be said—that almost anything can happen in history. Let us refuse to be intimidated by 'the inevitable', or discouraged by the elaborate constructions of Spengler and Toynbee, the laws they devise and impose.

On an extreme view, the study of history can be

alleged to have scant value—in the phrase of Gibbon only 'the record of the crimes and follies of humanity'. And it can be added that the 'lessons of history' are all too often either obvious or delusive. Yet Gibbon did not consider that the story of the past was wholly devoid of instruction.

Henry Adams said of history that it is 'in essence incoherent and immoral'.[22] None the less, in the phrase of Namier, a notable enemy of system and dogma, it can be described as an 'intelligible disorder'.[23] 'Intelligible' is the word. Our occupations are not inevitably condemned to futility or pessimism. History is discovery. It broadens the horizon and deepens the understanding. It is a liberal and liberating force.

With such words it is suitable for me to terminate, in gratitude and in good spirits, recalling that we are commemorating Dr. Whidden and that we owe the establishment of these lectures to the enlightened generosity of Mr. Fox.[24]

NOTES

1 M. L. Hansen, *The Atlantic Migration, 1667–1860* (1941), 41.

2 See the highly critical portrayal by the Virginian historian T. J. Wertenbaker, *The Puritan Oligarchy* (1947, reprint 1956).

3 S. E. Morison, *The Intellectual Life of Colonial New England* (1956), 17 f. The first edition of this book appeared as *The Puritan Pronaos* (1935).

4 The process is documented with detail and elegance by R. Pares, *Yankee and Creole* (1956).

5 cf. the account in T. J. Wertenbaker, op. cit.

6 For the origins and growth of this aristocracy see T. J. Wertenbaker, *Patrician and Plebeian in Virginia* (1910); *The Planters of Colonial Virginia* (1922); L. B. Wright, *The First Gentlemen of Virginia* (1940).

7 Between a half and a third of the white immigrants to Virginia before 1776 were convicts or indentured servants, according to C.

Bridenhaugh, *Myths and Realities. The Societies of the Colonial South* (1952), 7.

8 S. E. Morison, op. cit., 101 f.

9 Thus the poetess Anne Bradstreet (S. E. Morison, op. cit., 218 ff.), or the Virginian historian Robert Beverley (edited by L. B. Wright, 1947).

10 S. E. Morison, op. cit., 274 f.

11 What follows is based on the excellent book of W. L. Sachse, *The Colonial American in Britain* (1955).

12 W. L. Sachse, op. cit., 3 ff.

13 W. L. Sachse, op. cit., 47 ff.

14 For example, ' the smoak of this stinking town ' (cited by W. L. Sachse, op. cit., 23).

15 viz., to L. B. Namier, *England in the Age of the American Revolution* (1930), 272 ff.

16 L. B. Namier, op. cit., 267 ff.

17 Reproduced in the *Miscellaneous Works of Edward Gibbon Esq.*, I (1814), 204 f. Dated 24 October, 1767, it is the reply to Gibbon's letter of 4 October (C. E. Norton, *The Letters of Edward Gibbon*, I (1956), 218 f., Letter 78).

18 That thesis, which goes back to John Adams, has been firmly expounded by Clinton Rossiter, *Seedtime of the Republic* (1953).

19 Cited by A. S. Aiton, *Antonio de Mendoza, First Viceroy of New Spain* (1927), 51.

20 cf. C. H. van Tyne, *The Causes of the War of Independence* (1921), 213 ff.

21 It was the singular destiny of this, the most ' English ' of the American dynastic families, to be brought into clash with England in three successive generations (the two Presidents and the Minister in London during the Civil War). Cf. J. Truslow Adams, who was no relation, in *The Adams Family* (1930).

22 *The Education of Henry Adams* (Houghton Mifflin, n.d.), 301: ' in essence incoherent and immoral, history had either to be taught as such —or falsified.'

23 I regret that I cannot vouch for the origin of this maxim.

24 I was fortunate to have, and am happy to acknowledge, the most amicable help and guidance in new fields of study. My thanks go to Mr. B. Bailyn and Mr. G. H. Nadel of Harvard University, and to Professor Irving A. Leonard of Ann Arbor—and above all to Mr. Walter Muir Whitehill; and, on the other side of the Atlantic, to Mr. Richard Pares, Professor R. A. Humphreys and Mr. J. P. Cooper.

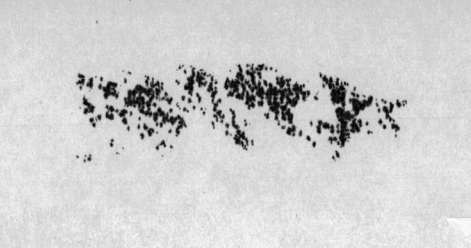